Pilgrim Children
Come to Plymouth

Pilgrim Children Come to Plymouth

By Ida DeLage

Drawings by Herman Vestal

GARRARD PUBLISHING COMPANY
CHAMPAIGN, ILLINOIS

Library of Congress Cataloging in Publication Data

DeLage, Ida.
  Pilgrim children come to Plymouth.

  SUMMARY: Depicts the Pilgrims' first year at
Plymouth, their hardships, their relations with the
Indians, and the first Thanksgiving celebration.
  1. Pilgrims (New Plymouth Colony)—Juvenile
literature. 2. Massachusetts—History—New Plymouth,
1620-1691—Juvenile literature. [1. Pilgrims (New
Plymouth Colony)] I. Vestal, Herman B. II. Title.
F68.D43   974.4'02   80-29180
ISBN 0-8116-6084-2

Pilgrim Children Come to Plymouth

It is moving day.
The Pilgrims are moving
from the ship Mayflower
to their new houses on the land.
The children climb down
into a small boat.
"Be careful," say the mothers.

The boat moves away from
the Mayflower.
Some of the Pilgrims
are still on the ship.
They wave good-bye.
When houses are built for them,
they can leave the Mayflower too.

The Pilgrims have come
from across the wide ocean.
They sailed away from England
on the little ship Mayflower
to this new land.
For many winter weeks
the Pilgrim children and mothers
have been living on the ship
near the land.
The Pilgrim fathers have been busy
building new houses
for everyone to live in.
At last some of the houses
are finished.
Today is the first moving day.

Now the boat reaches the land.
The children see a row
of little houses.
This is Plymouth Colony,
their new home.
The excited children
jump out of the boat.

"Come back!" call the fathers.
"Everyone must help to move."
The children carry boxes
and pots and blankets
to the new houses.

The children like the new houses.
"They are very little houses,"
they say.
"But it is better
to live in a little house
than to live on a ship."

There is one big house.

It is the Common House.

The Common House is the hospital
for sick Pilgrims.

It is also a meeting house.

On Sunday, it is the church.

The children peek
into the Common House.
They see some kegs
of gunpowder.
They see large baskets too.
"What are they?"
the children ask.

"They are Indian baskets,"
a Pilgrim father says.
"We found these baskets
filled with Indian corn.
We need corn
to plant in the spring.
Corn is good food.
If we do not have food,
we will starve.
We hope
the Indians are not angry
because we took the corn.
Some day,
we will pay the Indians
for this corn that we found."

The children run everywhere
and look at everything.
They see fields and woods.
"Look over here," calls Love.
"Here is a brook."

The fathers go hunting.
They bring back two ducks
and a fat goose.
Soon good soup
is cooking in the pots.

The Pilgrims have supper
by their fires.
The walls of the houses
keep out the wind and cold.
The Pilgrims are happy
in their new home,
Plymouth Colony.

All of the Pilgrims
go to church on Sunday
in the Common House.
The Pilgrim men carry guns.
"We will watch for Indians,"
they say.
But they do not see any Indians.

The Pilgrims sing and pray
and give thanks.
"We came across
the great, wide ocean.
We came to this new land
to be free.
We built our own church.
Now we can go to church
and pray
the way we want to.
We give thanks for our church
and for our freedom."
The Pilgrims go home for dinner.
Then they go back to church.
They sing and pray again.

The children are tired.

John makes a face.

Mary laughs, "Tee-hee!"

They get a tap-tap with the rod.

The Pilgrim children know

they must not laugh in church.

The winter is long and cold.
Many of the Pilgrims are sick.
Some of them die.
The Pilgrims dig graves at night
and cover them with snow.
They don't want Indians to see
how many Pilgrims have died.

One day
the hunters brought back
only one duck.
Everyone had to share it.
"We are still hungry,"
the children cry.
"Hush!" the mothers tell them.
"Be thankful for what we have."

The men work hard every day.
"Some of the Pilgrims
are still on the Mayflower,"
they say.
"We must make houses for them."

One day,
the children are picking up wood
to start the fires.
"Look!" they shout.
"Indians are looking at us!"
The Indians have painted faces.
They carry big bows and arrows.

The children run home so fast
they drop the wood.
The Pilgrims are afraid
the Indians will make war.
They get a big cannon
from the Mayflower.

The men shoot off the cannon,
BOOM!
"The Indians can hear
this big cannon,"
say the Pilgrims.
"Now they will be afraid
to make war upon us
with their bows and arrows."

At last

it is springtime in Plymouth.

The birds are singing.

The long, cold winter is over.

"Come on!" calls John.

"Let's have a race."

Suddenly,

the children stop running.

Coming down the street

is a tall Indian.

He has a big bow and arrow.

The Pilgrims hurry

out of their houses.

They are afraid.

What will the Indian do?

But the Indian smiles.
He lifts his hand,
and he says,
"Welcome!"

"I am Samoset,"
says the Indian.
Samoset tells the Pilgrims
all about the Indians
who live near them.
"The Big Chief Massasoit
wishes to see you," he says.

Samoset comes back again
with Big Chief Massasoit.
He brings his friend, Squanto,
and many Indian braves.
The Indians and the Pilgrims
smoke the peace pipe.
"We will always live
in peace together," they say.

Today, the last Pilgrims
are moving from the Mayflower.
The children clap their hands.
"Oh what lovely houses!
We never want to live
in a ship again."

The Mayflower is ready to leave.
The children stand on a hill.
"Good-bye, Mayflower!"
The wind puffs her sails.
The good little ship sails away,
back to England.

"Now," the Pilgrims say,
"it is time to plant our seeds.'
"I will show you
how to plant corn,"
says Squanto.
"First you make a trap
in the brook
to catch many little fish."

"Then," says Squanto,

"you dig a hole.

You put three fish in the hole.

Cover the fish with dirt.

Now put in five corn seeds.

Cover them with dirt.

This is how to plant corn."

Indians come to live
on the other side of the brook.
The Indian children
and the Pilgrim children
are friends.
"Come and play with us,"
the Indians say in sign talk.

Their Indian friends
show the Pilgrim children
where the best berries grow.
They show them
where to find nuts
and where the bees
hide their honey.

Summer days are happy days.
Now the Pilgrim children
are not afraid to play
in the woods.
They run in the sunshine.
They play in the brook.

The corn grows tall and strong.
So do the children.
The Indians show the Pilgrims
how to make baskets.
They show them
how to make moccasins.

The men have time now
to build better houses.
The new houses
are big and strong.

The Pilgrims pay the Indians
for the corn they found.
They pay them with knives
and pots and pretty beads.
The Indians are happy.
The Pilgrims are happy, too.

Now the leaves are turning
red and gold.
It is time to pick the corn.
Everyone helps.
"We are thankful
for this fine harvest,"
say the Pilgrims.

"We must give thanks together,"
the Pilgrims say.
"We shall have a harvest party.
We shall invite
Big Chief Massasoit and his braves."
The children run to invite
their Indian friends.

The men go hunting
for ducks and turkeys.
The women get out
their big cooking pots.
The happy children get wood
and carry water.
Oh what fun a party will be!

Many Indians come to the party.
They bring deer
and fruit and nuts.
The children eat and eat
until their tummies are full.
The Pilgrims and Indians
visit and play games.

The Indians
put on a dance.

The Pilgrims
put on a parade.

The Pilgrims pray,
"We give thanks
for our good food,
for our good homes,
for our good friends,
in Plymouth Colony."
THIS IS THE FIRST
THANKSGIVING.